Leonardo da Vinci (1452-1519) was born in Italy, the son of a gentleman of Florence. He made significant contributions to many different disciplines, including anatomy, botany, geology, astronomy, architecture, paleontology, and cartography.

He is one of the greatest and most influential painters of all time, creating masterpieces such as the *Mona Lisa* and *The Last Supper*. And his imagination led him to create designs for things such as an armored car, scuba gear, a parachute, a revolving bridge, and flying machines. Many of these ideas were so far ahead of their time that they weren't built until centuries later.

He is the original "Renaissance Man" whose genius extended to all five areas of today's STEAM curriculum: Science, Technology, Engineering, the Arts, and Mathematics.

You can find more information on Leonardo da Vinci in *Who Was Leonardo da Vinci?* by Roberta Edwards (Grosset & Dunlap, 2005), *Magic Tree House Fact Tracker: Leonardo da Vinci* by Mary Pope Osborne and Natalie Pope Bryce (Random House, 2009), and *Leonardo da Vinci for Kids: His Life and Ideas* by Janis Herbert (Chicago Review Press, 1998).

Little Leonardo's™

Fascinating World of ENGINEERING

Illustrated by
GREG PAPROCKI

Written by
BOB COOPER

GIBBS SMITH
TO ENRICH AND INSPIRE HUMANKIND

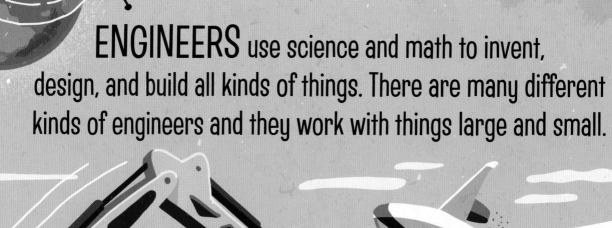

ENGINEERS use science and math to invent, design, and build all kinds of things. There are many different kinds of engineers and they work with things large and small.

Some design and build large structures like buildings, bridges, and dams.

Others work with tiny computer circuits or microscopic genes in the human body.

There are even engineers who design the SYSTEMS and PROCESSES that other engineers use to make things.

With their knowledge of physics and an understanding of how POWER is generated, MECHANICAL ENGINEERS design machines and mechanical systems.

These include all sorts of things people use and see every day, like refrigerators, air conditioners, elevators, airplanes, boats, and cars.

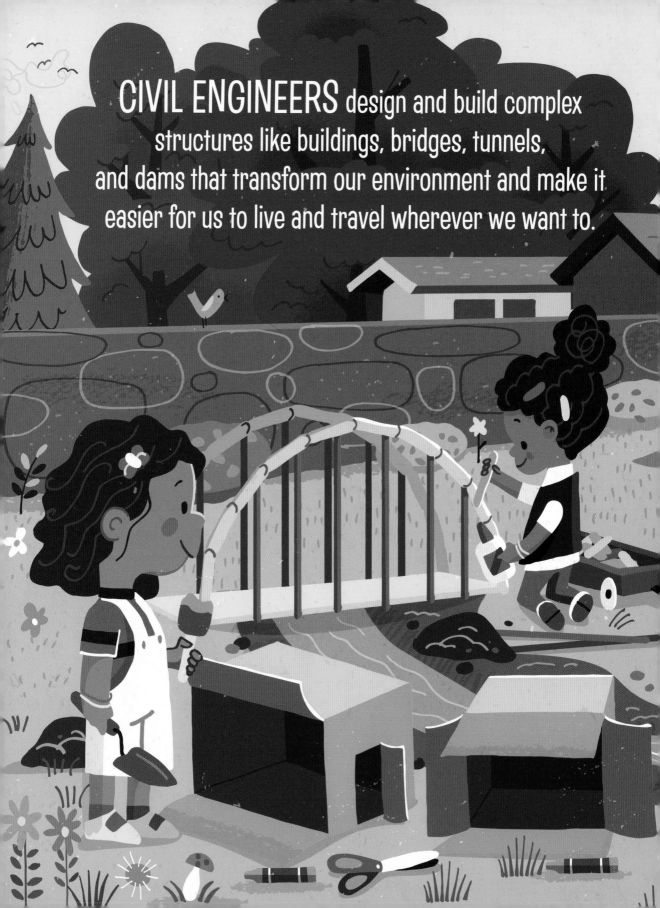

CIVIL ENGINEERS design and build complex structures like buildings, bridges, tunnels, and dams that transform our environment and make it easier for us to live and travel wherever we want to.

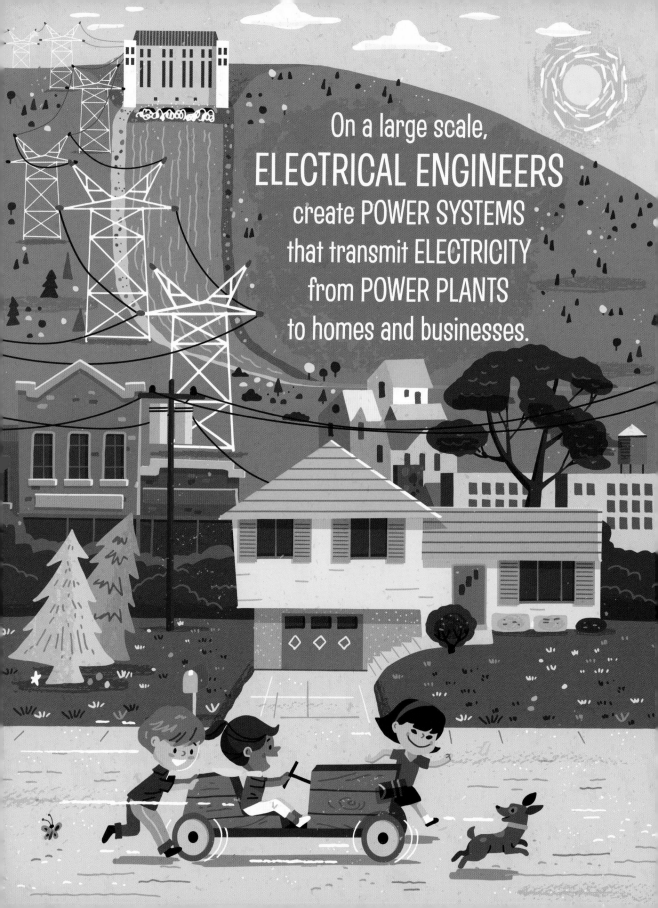

On a large scale,
ELECTRICAL ENGINEERS
create POWER SYSTEMS
that transmit ELECTRICITY
from POWER PLANTS
to homes and businesses.

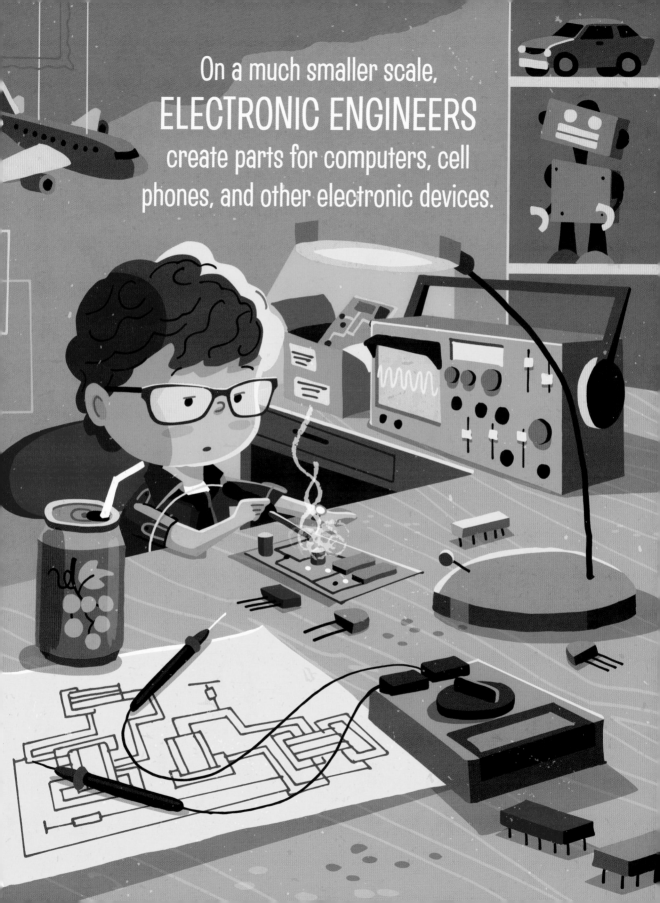

On a much smaller scale, **ELECTRONIC ENGINEERS** create parts for computers, cell phones, and other electronic devices.

COMPUTER ENGINEERS design, build, and test computer systems and their components, like CIRCUIT BOARDS and devices for DATA STORAGE.

They also design and build devices that allow
us to connect many computers together in a
COMPUTER NETWORK or communicate across the INTERNET.

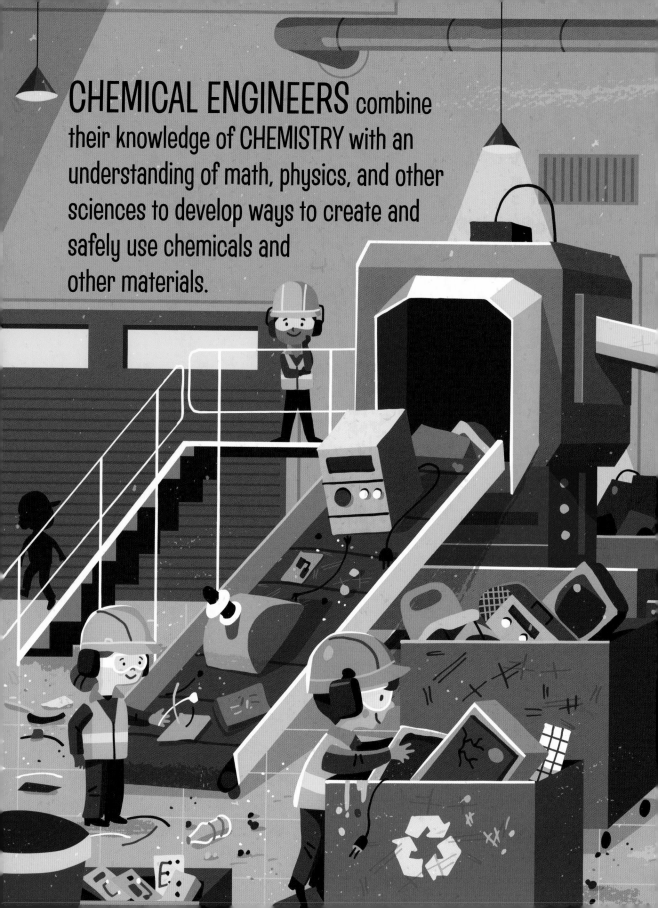

CHEMICAL ENGINEERS combine their knowledge of CHEMISTRY with an understanding of math, physics, and other sciences to develop ways to create and safely use chemicals and other materials.

There are types of garbage that can't be
easily RECYCLED. Using chemistry, some of it can
be changed into fuel and other useful products.

ASTRONAUTICAL ENGINEERS design
and build ROCKETS and SPACECRAFT that travel into SPACE.

Their designs must consider that objects move differently in the atmosphere at different altitudes, and are subject to different amounts of GRAVITY when traveling beyond the atmosphere.

BIOMEDICAL ENGINEERS create new medical technology by combining engineering with their knowledge of biology and other life sciences.

"Smart" artificial limbs will eventually provide nearly the same movement and reactions as a normal limb.

Engineers in the field of ROBOTICS have been working on creating a robot that can do all the same things a human can, including using ARTIFICIAL INTELLIGENCE to make decisions.

For example, by counting how many ticket takers there are and measuring how much time it takes for you to give them your ticket and get in the car, they can design ways to make the lines at your favorite theme park shorter or move more quickly.

SYSTEMS ENGINEERS study whole systems to try to make all their parts and processes work together in the best possible way.

It could be a complicated machine made up of thousands of parts, like a car. Or it could be a business with hundreds of people who create and sell products.

Many different kinds of engineers work to design things that make our lives better. Everywhere you look you'll find something that an engineer created.

What kind of an engineer would *you* like to be?

GLOSSARY

AERONAUTICAL ENGINEER (air-uh-NOT-ick-ull en-juh-NEAR): An engineer who designs and builds airplanes and other types of aircraft.

AIRPLANE: A vehicle with wings that flies through the air.

ARTIFICIAL INTELLIGENCE (art-uh-FISH-ull in-TELL-uh-jentz): The ability of certain machines like computers and robots to mimic human capabilities such as learning and problem solving.

ASTRONAUTICAL ENGINEER (as-truh-NOT-uh-cull en-juh-NEAR): An engineer who designs and builds rockets and other vehicles for space travel.

ATMOSPHERE (AT-muss-fear): The layer of air that surrounds the Earth.

BIOMEDICAL ENGINEER (by-oh-MED-ick-ull en-juh-NEAR): An engineer with knowledge of biology and medicine who helps with medical diagnoses and treatment, including creating devices such as prosthetic limbs and artificial organs.

CIRCUIT BOARD (SIR-cut board): A collection of tiny electronic components joined on a board; found in devices like cell phones and computers.

CHEMICAL ENGINEER (KEM-ick-ull en-juh-NEAR): An engineer who designs processes that convert chemicals, fuels, drugs, foods, and other materials into useful products.

CHEMISTRY (KEM-us-tree): The study of the basic structure of substances and materials, and how they interact, combine, and change.

CIVIL ENGINEER (SIV-ull en-juh-NEAR): An engineer who designs, builds, and maintains large structures like roads, dams, bridges, and buildings that fit in with our physical environment.

COMPUTER ENGINEER: An engineer who combines knowledge of electrical engineering and computer science to design computer hardware, software, operating systems, and networks.

COMPUTER NETWORK: A connected system of computers and other devices, like printers and routers, allowing files and applications to be shared. Also see INTERNET.

DATA STORAGE: Hard drives and other recording media, such as DVDs, that are used to retain digital data.

ELECTRICAL ENGINEER (uh-LECK-trick-ul en-juh-NEAR): An engineeer who applies the principles of electricity to the analysis and development of electrical systems and electronic devices.

ELECTRICAL POWER (uh-LECK-trick-ul POW-ur): Electricity that is collected and used to operate machines, lights, and other devices.

ELECTRICITY (uh-leck-TRIS-uh-tee): A basic interaction that occurs between atomic particles; when the particles are forced to move along a wire they create an ELECTRIC CURRENT, which can be used to produce electrical power.

ELECTRONIC ENGINEER (uh-leck-TRON-ick en-juh-NEAR): A type of electrical engineer who specializes in designing and building electronic devices.

ENGINEER (en-juh-NEAR): Someone who uses their knowledge of math, physics, and other sciences to design, build, and maintain machines, structures, systems, processes, or products.

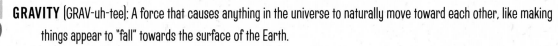

GRAVITY (GRAV-uh-tee): A force that causes anything in the universe to naturally move toward each other, like making things appear to "fall" towards the surface of the Earth.

INDUSTRIAL ENGINEER (in-DUST-real en-juh-NEAR): An engineer who designs systems and processes that improve a product's quality and eliminate wasted time and resources in making it.

INTERNET (IN-tur-net): A vast network that connects billions of computers and other electronic devices throughout the world.

MECHANICAL ENGINEER (muh-CAN-ick-ull en-juh-NEAR): An engineer who uses their knowledge of math, physics, and the properties of materials to design and build machines and other mechanical systems.

MECHANICAL POWER: The rate of work done by a mechanical device, such as the amount of HORSEPOWER generated by an engine.

POWER: Energy that can be collected and used to operate machines, lights, and other devices. The energy can come from various sources, such as water, wind, the sun, or electricity.

POWER PLANT: A generating station that provides electricity.

POWER SYSTEM: A network of equipment for distributing electrical power across a large area, including power plants, towers and poles, and wires.

PROCESS: Any planned set of actions that produces something or leads to some other result, like the process of choosing and paying for groceries at the supermarket.

RECYCLE (ree-SY-cull): To make something new from something that's already been used.

ROBOTICS (row-BOT-icks): The study of how to design, build, and operate ROBOTS.

ROCKET: A vehicle designed to fly in both atmosphere and space, with an engine powered by the explosive release of gases created from burning fuel.

SPACE: All of the area beyond the Earth's atmosphere, including the Sun, Moon, and other planets and stars.

SPACECRAFT: A vehicle used for travel in space.

SYSTEM: A group of things that are designed to work together.

SYSTEMS ENGINEER: An engineer who designs, builds, and operates systems.

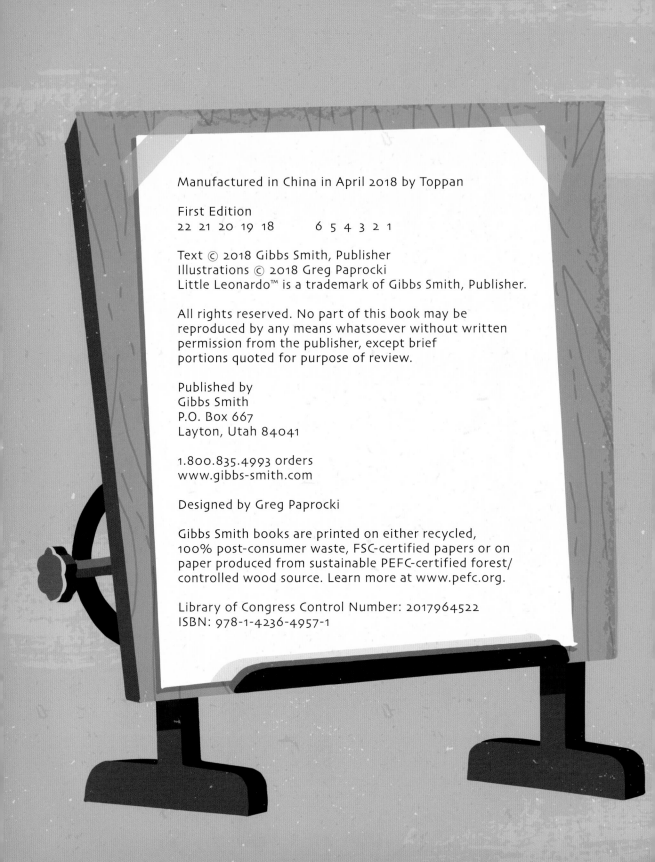

Manufactured in China in April 2018 by Toppan

First Edition
22 21 20 19 18   6 5 4 3 2 1

Published by
Gibbs Smith
P.O. Box 667
Layton, Utah 84041

1.800.835.4993 orders
www.gibbs-smith.com

Designed by Greg Paprocki

Gibbs Smith books are printed on either recycled,
100% post-consumer waste, FSC-certified papers or on
paper produced from sustainable PEFC-certified forest/
controlled wood source. Learn more at www.pefc.org.

Library of Congress Control Number: 2017964522
ISBN: 978-1-4236-4957-1

Some engineers of note . . .

Archimedes (ca. 287–212 BCE)

He's recognized as the greatest engineer of all time, and had a major influence on mathematics, physics, engineering, and astronomy. He was the first to apply math principles to physical phenomena, explaining such things as how the lever works. His discoveries and inventions include the screw pump, a simple odometer, compound pulley systems, and improvements to battle machines like the catapult.

Lewis Latimer (ca. 1848–1928)

He taught himself drafting and electrical engineering principles, and found work with both Alexander Graham Bell and Thomas Edison. He helped popularize Edison's light bulb by inventing a method of producing the carbon filaments used in the bulbs, making them cheaper to manufacture and more efficient to use. He's also credited with several other inventions, including improvements to the air conditioner.

Nikola Tesla (1856–1943)

As a mechanical engineer and physicist, he made significant contributions in many fields, including the design of the AC electrical supply system and important discoveries in radar and X-ray technology. He devised plans for a worldwide wireless communication system that was never developed because of a lack of financing.

Lillian Moller Gilbreth (1878–1972)

She was an American psychologist and industrial engineer, as well as a mother of twelve. She performed time-and-motion studies to determine more efficient ways to perform household and workplace tasks. She was among the first to recognize the harmful effects of fatigue and stress in the workplace, leading to the study of ergonomics. Her family's well-organized life was the basis for three movies, a stage play, and a musical based on the book *Cheaper by the Dozen,* written by two of her children.

Katherine Johnson (1918–)

After becoming the first black woman in West Virginia University's graduate math program, she became one of NASA's "human computers" in the late 1950s. She was part of the team responsible for calculating orbital trajectories for American astronauts in the 1960s. This included calculating John Glenn's landmark orbits around the Earth in 1962 and Apollo 11's moon landing in 1969. Her story, and those of other pioneering black women at NASA, was brought to the big screen in the 2016 Oscar-nominated movie *Hidden Figures.*

Ellen Ochoa (1958–)

An American engineer and astronaut, she became the first Hispanic woman to travel into space aboard the space shuttle *Discovery* in 1993. As an engineer, she developed optical systems for information processing, automated space exploration, and an inspection system to find defects in materials. She became the first woman director of NASA's Johnson Space Center in 2012.

ENGINEERING